"Authorship is such a bore"

SLEEPING PARTNERS

SLEEPING PARTNERS

Cracker and Micky: Two Dogs with a Tale

by

Cecil Aldin

Introduced by Roy Heron

Souvenir Press

First published 1929 by Eyre and Spottiswoode Limited

This edition © Souvenir Press 2000

This edition published 2000 by
Souvenir Press Ltd.,
43 Great Russell Street, London WC1B 3PA

Reprinted 2001

Cecil Aldin illustrations © Anthony C. Mason, renewed 1995

Introduction © Roy Heron 2000

ISBN 0 285 63592 1

Printed in Italy

Aldin with Cracker and Micky

INTRODUCTION

by Roy Heron
Cecil Aldin's biographer

Few people are lucky enough to experience that blend of sagacity, loyalty and fun that turns a dog into something very special. Such was Cracker: a white bull terrier, with a black spot over one eye and comical ways, who became the most famous dog in the world through portraits of him in magazines and newspapers, and a dozen or so best-selling books in which he featured in the 1920s and early 1930s.

Cracker was the bosom pal and leading 'professional' model of the celebrated artist Cecil Aldin (1870–1935), who illustrated more than 150 books, and was supreme in his portrayal of dogs.

In his later years, and increasingly troubled by arthritis, Aldin concentrated more and more on drawing and painting dogs. He gathered together a wonderfully mixed pack which he called 'the professionals' – the 'amateurs' being the many casual visitors whose portraits had been commissioned or who were there by invitation simply because Aldin liked the look of them. He regarded the professionals as part of his firm, with Cracker as the senior member of the board and as much a star of the illustrated page as Rin Tin Tin was of the silver screen.

Even the finest performers need the right setting to give of their best. It helps to have a sympathetic but lugubrious straight man to show off their quicksilver brilliance. Cracker had the perfect arena: a 60-foot-long former Army hut which Aldin used as a studio, and which adjoined the kennels of the South Berks Foxhounds. The studio was always crowded with dogs of all kinds, and when Cracker was holding court, there too was his boon companion and straight man, an Irish wolfhound called Micky, reputed to be the third largest dog in Britain and generally stretched full length on a sofa. So good-natured was the wolfhound that Cracker used him as a mattress, with just the mildest of protests from Micky when the bull terrier imposed his 60-pound weight on his more delicate anatomical regions. And so the pair became not only members of Aldin's board, but Sleeping Partners, hence the title of this series of drawings made over many months and published in book form, with just one-word captions, for the dogs were so well known that explanations were regarded as superfluous. These drawings, together with commissioned pastel portraits, prints and dry point etchings confirmed the growing opinion that Aldin not only created marvellous pictures but captured the very soul of a dog.

Aldin's introduction to Cracker and Micky had been completely by chance. He and his wife, Rita, were having tea with a group of friends at the Berkshire home of the legendary Mrs Florence Nagle, the international judge and breeder of Irish wolfhounds. There were several wolfhounds in the room and Rita persuaded her husband to buy one, Micky, then a three-month-old puppy. Another guest said she had bred a most captivating bull terrier, the same age as Micky, and they would make an ideal pair. Her offer was declined, but she persisted, saying her bull terrier was the most comic-looking puppy that ever whelped, with an adorable black spot over one eye. Aldin bought the puppy unseen, to be sent to him the following week. Cracker and Micky immediately became friends. They slept together, played together and were educated together.

In all their activities, Cracker was the undisputed leader, a friend to all, human and canine, and, like any top-class heavyweight, he had no reason to prove his strength. Would-be antagonists took one look at his powerful jaws and massive body and, more often than not, changed their minds. Should another dog challenge him, Cracker usually reacted by swinging his great hindquarters round and knocking his opponent flat. Then Cracker would stand over his floored adversary with his tail revving and a grin on his face that seemed to say, 'No hard feelings.'

Aldin disliked fixing his models in artificial poses. He spent hour after hour in the studio, smoking his pipe and waiting for the dogs to relax into interesting postures. He would start his drawing with the eyes – the key to a dog's character.

His daughter, Gwen, sometimes watched as the drawings for *Sleeping Partners* took shape. 'Every evening, he would sit with a notebook and pencil in hand, ready for some lightning sketch as the two dogs arranged themselves comfortably on the sofa,' she said. 'The bull terrier was always on top, but sometimes so precariously placed that it was only a matter of moments before he slipped!'

Aldin believed in kindly discipline and had a daily routine of work, play and obedience exercises which became as familiar to Cracker, Micky and co. as it was to their master. The highlight was afternoon tea, when the dogs followed Aldin into the house and lay in a semi-circle in front of a tiered cake stand. During tea, Rita Aldin threw small pieces of cake or bread and butter, to land precisely between the front legs of each dog, as its name was called. Aldin had copied from Lord Lonsdale the trick of persuading dogs to lie down in particular places during the owners' mealtimes. It did not always work, for Micky sometimes infiltrated his ungainly body beneath a low table. When the wolfhound rose, he took the table on his back, with disastrous results.

Micky was not averse to embarrassing his master in front of visitors. 'A tea party was in progress,' a guest, the author and poet, Patrick Chalmers, recalls. 'Among the silver and occasional tables was a high tier table and on the top tier was a big, white-sugar birthday cake, about as big, it seemed as two cheeses and a millstone. Micky lounged up to the cake. He took it entire into his tremendous jaws; he crunched it twice and swallowed it. No one seemed surprised but Aldin avoided my eye and, out of consideration for the one perfect illustrator and disciplinarian, I did not seek his.'

Cracker, despite his great bulk, became firm friends with a lamb (a childhood pet of Dorian Williams, the showjumping commentator and writer) and could be seen ponderously trying to out-gambol it. The lamb would follow Cracker everywhere. Each morning, for several weeks, either the lamb called for Cracker at the cottage where Aldin was staying or the dog sought out his woolly friend, then off they would go.

When his health declined, Aldin, his wife and their dogs moved to Majorca on medical advice. A regular flow of books and features in *The Illustrated London News*, *The Sketch* and *The New York Times* kept the dogs in the public eye. They received fan mail from all over the world; famous people called on them and their afternoon tea parties became a holiday attraction.

Sadly, because of his great size and heavy coat, Micky never became acclimatised and he died of heart failure a year after arriving on the island. And, in January 1935, Aldin suffered a fatal heart attack on what was to have been a nostalgic visit to England.

At the very time Cecil Aldin breathed his last in The London Clinic, Cracker, 1,000 miles away, set up a heart-rending howl, such as he had never made before and could not be quietened. Not for many hours did news of Aldin's death arrive. The incident was confirmed by Rita Aldin, who said there was no way the dog could have known anything was amiss, except by some canine sixth sense.

Cracker, then approaching his tenth birthday, was too old for the trauma of quarantine, which a return to England would have entailed. Rita said she could not desert him, especially since Cecil had made thousands of pounds out of him and Micky, and they were the best known dogs in the world.

When Cracker died in 1937, two years and seven months after his master, his passing was reported on cinema newsreels and the radio, and in newspapers in many countries. The event attracted editorial comment, and obituary notices appeared in *The Times* and *The Morning Post*, making thousands of readers pause over their breakfast:

Cracker, the bull terrier, for many years the beloved companion and favourite model of the late Cecil Aldin, died July 31st in Mallorca. Deeply mourned.

Cracker was reunited with his old friend, Micky, and the other professional models in the dogs' cemetery which Aldin had made in the studio garden at Camp de Mar.

SUPPLICATION

AMALGAMATION

SEPARATION

PROBATION

GRATIFICATION

RESIGNATION

ELEVATION

UNDULATION

TREPIDATION

RELAXATION

AGGLOMERATION

EXECRATION

EXCOMMUNICATION

PROPITIATION

RECONCILIATION

APPROBATION

TOLERATION

CONSOLIDATION

GRAVITATION

D——NATION

"It's a book about us"

"But my name comes first"